FIRE FIGHTERS

BY NORMA SIMON
ILLUSTRATED BY PAM PAPARONE

Harcourt

Orlando   Boston   Dallas   Chicago   San Diego

Visit *The Learning Site!*
www.harcourtschool.com

This edition is published by special arrangement with
Simon & Schuster Books for Young Readers,
Simon & Schuster Children's Publishing Division.

Grateful acknowledgment is made to
Simon & Schuster Books for Young Readers,
Simon & Schuster Children's Publishing Division for permission to reprint
Fire Fighters by Norma Simon, illustrated by Pam Paparone. Text copyright © 1995
by Norma Simon; illustrations copyright © 1995 by Pam Paparone.

Printed in the United States of America

ISBN 0-15-314271-5

2 3 4 5 6 7 8 9 10   060   02 01 00

For our brave and caring
Wellfleet fire fighters
—N.S.

To my Uncle Sonny, a courageous
fire captain for many years
—P.P.

When the fire bell r-i-n-g-s,
fire fighters stop
whatever they are doing.

Slide down the fire pole
one after the other,
pull on heavy pants,
pull on heavy boots,
into the coats,
on with the hats,
and up on the trucks they go.

Open the firehouse doors.
Start the engines.
They're off!

Cars hear the sirens
wailing, wailing.
Pull to the side of the road and stop!
Let the fire trucks roar by.

Fire fighters work hard.
Fighting fires is their work.

Out shoots the water!
Up go the ladders.
Up go the fire fighters.

Fire fighters wear masks
to help them breathe
through the smoke.
They search upstairs
and downstairs
to get everyone out.

After the fire fighters
put out the fire,
with everyone safe and sound and warm,
their hard work is done.

Time to look around.
Time to ask questions.
How did this fire start to burn?
Fire fighters search
all around the fire,
poking, checking
for answers to their questions.

They pack up ladders and tools.
Up go the hoses into the trucks.
They drive back slowly.
No sirens now.

Down from the trucks
come the tired fire fighters.

Pants and coats go up on hooks.
Boots stand
in a straight row.
Hats sit on a long hat shelf.
Everything back in its place.

It's time to rest.
Fire fighters eat in the firehouse kitchen.

Then it is time to wash the fire trucks and
wind up the hoses.
Time to clean the breathing masks
and check every tank.
Make everything ready
to fight the next fire.

There are always fire fighters in the firehouse,
night or day,
ready to go
when the fire bell r-i-n-g-s.

Open the firehouse doors.
Start the engines.
They're on their way!